Burgh Island
and
Bigbury Bay

Chips Barber and Judy Chard

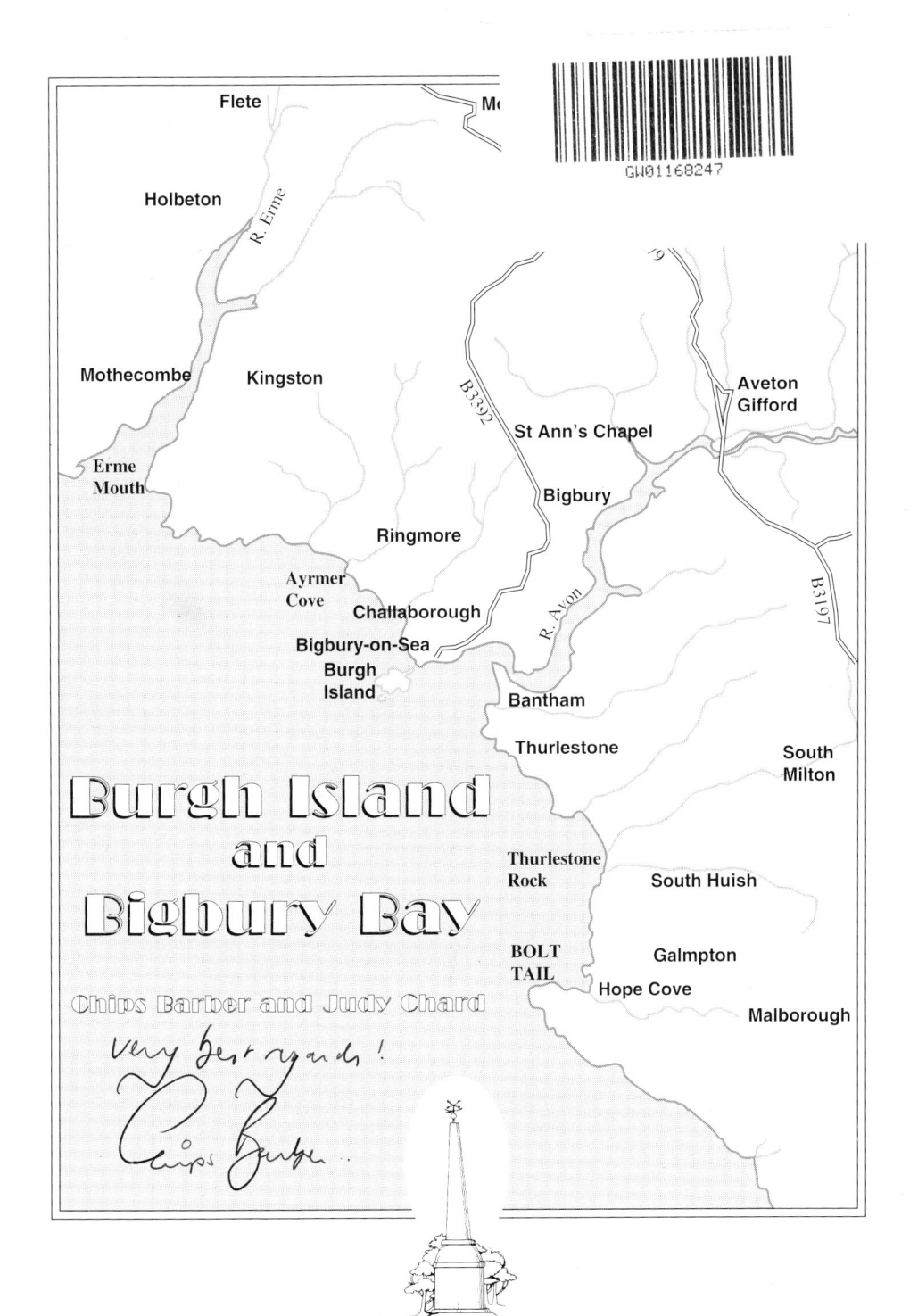

OBELISK PUBLICATIONS

OTHER BOOKS BY THE AUTHORS:
Tales of the Teign, Chips Barber and Judy Chard
Tales of the Unexplained in Devon, Judy Chard
Haunted Happenings in Devon, Judy Chard
Around & About Salcombe, Chips Barber
Around & About Seaton and Beer, Chips Barber
Around & About Sidmouth, Chips Barber
Around & About Teignmouth, Chips Barber
The Lost City of Exeter, Chips Barber
Diary of a Dartmoor Walker, Chips Barber
Diary of a Devonshire Walker, Chips Barber
The Great Little Dartmoor Book, Chips Barber
The Great Little Exeter Book, Chips Barber
Made in Devon, Chips Barber and David FitzGerald
Dartmoor in Colour, Chips Barber
Dark & Dastardly Dartmoor, Sally and Chips Barber
Exeter in Colour, Chips Barber
Torbay in Colour, Chips Barber
The Ghosts of Exeter, Sally and Chips Barber
The Great Little Totnes Book, Chips Barber and Bill Bennett
Ten Family Walks on Dartmoor, Sally and Chips Barber
The Great Little Plymouth Book, Chips Barber
Plymouth in Colour, Chips Barber
Weird & Wonderful Dartmoor, Sally and Chips Barber
Ghastly and Ghostly Devon, Sally and Chips Barber
Dawlish and Dawlish Warren, Chips Barber
The South Hams, Chips Barber
Torquay / Paignton / Brixham, Chips Barber
Ten Family Walks in East Devon, Sally and Chips Barber
For further details, please contact us at the address below or telephone (0392) 468556

ACKNOWLEDGEMENTS
Title page sketch map by Sally Barber
All photographs by or belonging to Chips Barber
Front cover: Burgh Island. Back cover: (top) Thurlestone Rock (bottom) Hope Cove

First published in 1988, reprinted in 1990 (ISBN 0 946651 25 6)
Revised edition printed in 1993 (ISBN 0 946651 80 9)
by Obelisk Publications, 2 Church Hill, Pinhoe, Exeter, Devon
Designed by Chips and Sally Barber
Typeset by Sally Barber
Printed in Great Britain by
Sprint Print Co Ltd, Okehampton Place, Exeter

© **Chips Barber and Judy Chard 1993**
All Rights Reserved

Burgh Island and Bigbury Bay

Burgh Island

Anyone visiting the island must be fascinated by its unique ferry, a sea tractor created specifically for the difficult navigation of the channel, driven for many years by 'Jimbo', who looked every inch a man of the sea with curly side whiskers and beard. A specially designed vehicle was necessary as violent pincer-like effects caused by the incoming tide around the island, and its slender link with the mainland, have always made the use of boats for transport highly hazardous. Although there is a ridge of fairly hard sand across the causeway to Burgh Island at low tide, the driver needs to know exactly what he is doing, as it varies. It is not advisable to try to drive a car across. Every year several are inevitably lost, they get stuck and the incoming tide covers them before they can be towed out!

It was many years ago in the days when Tom and Sue Waugh owned the island, which they did for twenty years, that Tom watched with growing dismay the rather clanging progress of the twenty-year-old track ferry by which the island and its hotel were served from the mainland. Tom contacted Beares of Newton Abbot, a firm well used to dealing with unusual orders. H. W. Glover put on his thinking cap and, after some consultation with Tom's personal friend, R. F. Jackson, the vehicle we see today emerged and it is still coping valiantly with all that is demanded of it. When full it carries thirty-five to forty people, weighs ten tons when laden and will work in up to seven feet of water. It trundles along at four miles an hour on firm sand, and at its heart, a Fordson six cylinder diesel developing eighty plus horsepower with an hydraulic pump attached powers it. This really is the key to the whole enterprise because this power centre supplies drive to each of four hydraulic motors housed in the wheel hubs. Tom Waugh and Beares had a few words with Dunlop who supplied RT 40 flotation tyres to aid the stability of the machine.

The sea monster spans twelve feet at the rear wheels, those in front have a ten foot track and are hydraulically steered to a maximum of ten degrees either way. All the metal work has been protected from weather and sea by anti-corrosion coatings and paint. The wheels are secured behind layers of zinc, aluminium and vinyl. In the design the question of both firm traction on high and dry sand as well as grip and weight on immersed sand arose and thus they decided on pneumatics.

However most mechanical forms of transport are prone to breakdown at some time and this unique sea monster chose an inopportune moment for a rare engine failure. On 5 August 1971, with a complement of thirteen passengers, it embarked on its three hundred yard crossing in what was later reported as 'difficult conditions'. At a mid point in the journey it broke down and, amidst much excitement and no small degree of anxiety, the Bantham Inshore Rescue Boat was called. Its prompt arrival was greeted with great joy because the sea tractor was taking quite a battering from the waves and was rocking about in the heavy sea. Fortunately the passengers were shuttled back to the mainland and the only damage done was to the rescue boat.

This adventure on the high sea may never have occurred at all if a proposed development had taken place in 1962; the island had been sold for about £110,000 and great changes were envisaged. 'Arndale' would take visitors and guests to the island on an aerial ropeway! A double cable would stretch the nine hundred feet from the mainland to the island and along it would pass fourteen cabins each capable of carrying four persons. In addition to this, shops, studios, a restaurant, a new cottage development, several stone built villas and even a skin diving and water ski base was considered. There must be something in the salt air of Burgh Island that gives people and planners fanciful ideas.

'The Jolly Roger' was once a familiar object with visitors to the island between the 1930s and the early 1970s. This was an old vessel that stood on timbers on the rocks above the high water mark and was used for a variety of purposes at different times. It is believed that the 'Jolly Roger' was a hooker, a fishing smack, built about 1920. Between the wars it was brought to the island and heaved up into position where it was turned initially into a cocktail bar. Following the Second World War it was converted into a honeymoon suite and could no doubt have told some amazing stories! But when it lost its charm it was used to accommodate temporary staff. In its last days it acted as a tea room but its timbers had become rotten and riddled with woodworm so it was decided to burn it on the beach in March 1970.

The early history of Burgh Island is as fascinating as its enchantment and magic is today. At one time it was known as St Michael's, named after the ancient chapel that once stood on the top, although now there are no remains to be seen. It then became known as la Burgh, in the fifteenth century it became Burrow or Burrough, and eventually it became known by its present name.

St Michael the Archangel is the patron saint of mariners, and his medieval chapel also acted as a beacon and warning to ships when a light was placed on the tower in stormy weather. William Camden wrote of it: "Where Avon's waters with sea are mixt, St Michael's on a rock is fixt."

An old document, written in 1755, describes the dimensions of this small chapel – presumably the person who surveyed it had left his precise measuring tools on the mainland, for it is given as five paces long and four paces broad! There were windows in the south and east walls.

The present ruin on the top of the island is the remains of a huer's or caller's hut. The huer signalled the approach of shoals of pilchards, glistening in the summer sunlight, to waiting fishermen on the shore. However, according to Mr Fox, who wrote a book about the Kingsbridge district in 1874, the hut was built by his grandfather for picnic parties visiting the island!

The pilchards caught as a result of the huer's warning were put in the curing cellars of the various buildings on the island, then the oil was extracted and exported to the Mediterranean. The flesh was sold to the mainland farmers as meal so that often the fields facing Burgh Island shone silver under the sun.

Few visitors to Bigbury Bay and Burgh Island today would imagine that in the immediate neighbourhood there was such a large fishing industry, giving employment to so many people. It has been suggested that the rights for fishing were originally granted as far back as medieval times by the Priors of Buckfast Abbey.

The movements of the pilchard shoals in the past were predictable and this quote from Mr Couch of the Penzance Natural History and Antiquarian Society in 1847 explains how they got to Bigbury Bay.

"*The main body retires for the winter into deep water, to the westward of the Scilly Isles. About the middle of Spring they rise from the depths of the ocean, and consort together in small shoals, which, as the season advances, unite into larger ones, and*

Burgh Island and Bigbury Bay

towards the end of July or beginning of August, combine in one mighty host, and advance towards the land in such amazing numbers as to discolour the water as far as the eye can reach. They strike the land generally to the north of Cape Cornwall, where a detachment turns to the NE, and constitutes the summer fishing of St Ives; but the bulk of the fish passes between Scilly and Land's End, and entering the British Channel, follows the windings of the shore as far as Bigbury Bay and The Start.

"*It is said in Moore's* Devon *that many years since a quantity of pilchards, enough to produce about £7,000, were taken in Bigbury Bay but of later years the fishing seasons have been less successful.*"

The fishermen used seine nets from small boats on the west side of the island, and on one occasion, during the middle of the last century, six nets worked the area bringing in 1,000 hogshead of fish, each containing about 2,000 pilchards, a record catch. The dictionary states "hogshead – formation obscure – is a measure of capacity containing 52½ imperial gallons, a large cask or butt."

Seine fishing took place along most of the Devon coast at one time. A net was spread over the side of a boat in a half circle to trap the fish, towed to the shore and pulled in. Sometimes in rough weather specially trained Newfoundland dogs, a practice common in South Devon, were sent out to catch ropes and bring them back to the men and women waiting on the shore to pull in the boats. The pilchards were sold on the beach for one shilling per hundred. Sometimes forty horses and carts would be waiting to take away the catch for sale in the South Hams and as far away as Plymouth. There was even a company formed locally, 'The Bigbury Bay Company,' who possessed the necessary equipment for pilchard fishing, and cellars for the cure of the fish at Challaborough and at the Warren, from whence they were shipped in hogsheads for the Mediterranean market.

All that is left to remind us of this industry is the Pilchard Inn on the island, an industry that was the livelihood of generations of local people. It seems that it declined shortly after the middle of the last century, partly because there was insufficient labour to cope, and partly because of the competition from deep sea fishing. With the disappearing shoals, many local, poorer people were deprived of an important part of their diet.

The Inn dates back to the fourteenth century, a time when a monastic community lived here grazing sheep. Probably it was originally built as a rest house offering other services such as a shop, and there was a large building where the hotel now stands, probably the monastery.

The Inn is unspoilt and the following quote comes from an old *'Guide to the Glorious South Hams of Devon'*, unfortunately undated and with no name of its writer:

"Burgh Island is steeped in folk lore of the dim past, the one time haunt of pirates and smugglers led by none other than the notorious Tom Crocker. An island of romance, adventure and treasure. Tom Crocker, Prince of Smugglers, evaded capture for many years, until eventually he was trapped and seized by the customs men and shot outside the Inn. A pirate flag and carving bearing the likeness of Crocker, both of which can be seen in the Pilchard, commemorate the event. Gone are the smugglers, gone are the pirates; the 'bold bad men' who come ashore today come in search of the greatest treasure of modern days – health and rest."

Sadly for us, gone too is the pirate flag, believed to have disappeared during the war when the Ministry of Defence took over the island. But Tom Crocker's face (complete with pipe) can still be seen, in profile, in the stones beside the fireplace. On the opposite side of the fireplace is said to be the effigy of the excise man who shot Tom Crocker. According to Tony Porter, the present owner of the island, there is a big flat rock where it is believed the smugglers landed their booty. It is possible as it's like a table, and one could pull a boat alongside. In the cove there is a cave that has collapsed. There are stories of a passage that came in under the island to the pub, or the cottage next door. Tony Porter understands that in years gone by people have tried to get into the cave, but two men died on one occasion when it fell in on them!

There are stories that Tom Crocker's ghost stays close to his old 'haunts' and, at one time, his ghostly wanderings were always noted on or about the 14 August, the anniversary of his death. On these occasions, not only did he rattle doors and cause mischief, but it seems he would walk all over the island, presumably stalking his hidden booty. Until 1939 a group of people regularly visited the island on this anniversary and dressed up in smugglers' costume to make Tom feel more at home! Tony Porter said that, like many people, he and his wife 'pooh poohed' the idea until one night, when they came back from holiday, they saw both doors of the pub opening! They were completely alone on the island, and the tide was in so no one could have come across.

The late Jimbo, once the driver of the famous tractor, confirmed this with a similar story of his own sighting. It was when he had been working on the island for about eleven years and he was in the pub one evening after work. There was no one on the island but himself. He had the keys to lock up when he finished, and had put on one little light, shut the doors and was sat by the window. Suddenly the door opened and closed. He said, "It's not easy, you have to pull a rope and the latch, it won't just open if you push it or the wind gets behind it. No way." On other occasions, Ron Bell, who had worked here for many years, was with him. He had a boxer dog and they used to do exactly the same thing at 6 o'clock each evening when they finished work – they'd go into the pub for a pint and the dog always went to the pub with them. If at any time Tom Crocker was around, the dog would come down the drive from the hotel, stop, go back, run round to the back of the pub, and wouldn't go near the corner where Tom was shot. One night they decided to put the dog on a lead but there was no way they could make him join them. The two men were not exactly weak, but that dog put down his four feet like four wheel brakes – and eventually they had to let him off the lead and he waited outside.

A collie dog was also known to react in a strange way. Inside on the right there is a trestle seat and at certain times the dog would go there and just stand and bark with his hackles up, nothing would move him, he stood absolutely rigid.

Apart from Tom Crocker and the inn, Jimbo believed there were other ghostly happenings. He once walked along the corridor of the top floor of the hotel and felt a tap on the shoulder; he experienced a really deadly cold feeling down his spine. He claimed there was a lady, a frequent visitor, who said she actually saw a ghost in that area – a white apparition.

Jimbo lived in the area for many years and, although he originally came to drive the tractor, he became a 'Jack of all trades'.

There is a stuffed parrot in the pub, referred to as 'Captain Laura' but was always called George in his 'squawking' days before he was bereft of life. He was kept in a large cage and fed gin and orange in his water. He loved his tipple and used bad language if he didn't get it! One night perhaps he had a drop too much for he just keeled over and died. However, he was over sixty years old!

In the early part of this century, George Chirgwin, who used to black his face and wear a patch over one eye, and was known in the Music Halls as the White Eyed Kaffir, bought the island and built himself a wooden house, which still stands near the hotel – he also brought top film actors and actresses of the day with him.

Burgh Island was once a 'jet-set' paradise, although that expression had not been invented in 1929 when Archibald Nettlefold built the hotel. It was more a luxury guest house for his business associates and friends, typical of the era of the 'Great Gatsby' and 'Brideshead Revisited' with its palm court roof covered with coloured Art Deco

glass, and a pool with gold tiles overhung with ferns and filled with goldfish.
  In the enormous ballroom famous dance bands blared out and flappers from London swarmed down as guests. It boasted a casino and was known as the English Monte Carlo.

Harry Roy provided a resident band in the shape of the Mayfair Four. He was famous not only for his band, but also for his marriage to Princess Pearl, one of the flamboyant daughters of Charles Vyner, the White Rajah of Sarawak who died in 1973. He is buried at Sheepstor on Dartmoor where Burrator House was presented to his ancestor, James Brooke, the first White Rajah of Sarawak.

There is a natural sea pool known as the Mermaid Pool where Archibald had the gaps filled in so it remained full of sea water even at low tide. In the centre was a dais or platform that, during the day was used for diving, and at night it was floodlit. The band would row across and play romantic music for dancing. Cars and chauffeurs were left in a special building on the mainland so nothing should intrude on the privacy of the guests. Archie's wife was a concert singer so it is not surprising to record that many of the visitors to the hotel were from the world of show biz.

The present owners of the island, Beatrice and Tony Porter, are obsessed with the Art Deco period, and have restored the hotel to its former glory. Perhaps one of the most interesting things that Archibald Nettlefold did was to install the Ganges Bar, which Tony has worked on most successfully to restore. It is transom shaped with the original ship's rudder attached outside. The ceiling is supported by the stem post from the top gun deck. HMS *Ganges* was the last sailing vessel commissioned by the British Navy, built in Bombay in 1819, launched in November 1821, commissioned at Portsmouth in 1823, and eventually broken up in Plymouth 1929. The post stands complete with epitaph and Tony has a whole collection of memorabilia, apart from the cabin and the rudder. They once had the wheel itself, but that has unfortunately been stolen.

During the Second World War the island was taken over by the Ministry of Defence. Tony has met one of the people who was in command here at the time, who has written an account of his memories for his family. He sent Tony an extract about some of the things that happened. He said there were tank traps and an organised cross fire of mortar bombs if anyone tried to land, a gun emplacement and a store for ammunition. On one occasion, when some of the 'top brass' came to inspect the island, he was told to fire a mortar bomb to drop exactly half way between where the staff car was standing on the mainland, and himself, to prove the accuracy of his firing. He succeeded but it was pretty tricky, only a tiny error and it could have been fatal! When the officers came over one of them turned out to be Alanbrooke, Chief of Imperial General Staff (1941-6). There were rumours too that Churchill and Eisenhower met here.

At one time the hotel belonged to Lady Anderson who owned a chain of hotels, and made this her flagship. This was when the hotel was really in its prime and to stay here cost £5 a day for full board, which sounds remarkably cheap until we remember that the average working wage was £3 a week!

In 1968 it was converted into self-catering flats, and in the early 1980s Landstone Estates of London bought the island intending to turn it into a luxury time share holiday homes complex. The idea never reached fruition and it was then Tony and Beatrice Porter came into the picture.

They were looking for a house and a business by the sea. They heard that Burgh Island was up for sale and dropped everything to come and look. It was November, the weather was cold but sunny, and as soon as they saw it, they knew they had to have it. Tony sees it as 'the Great Escape' for people working under pressure in busy city life who might go to Health Farms, although they don't really want to lose weight and have face packs, they really want just to 'get away from it all'. They have created for others a holiday that they themselves could never find but were always looking for.

Obviously much of the atmosphere of magic and enchantment arises because of the people who have at some time visited here, for the fame of Burgh Island spread world wide. Turner, the painter, stayed here to immortalise its beauty on canvas. Noel Coward, suffering from stress and exhaustion, came for three days and stayed for three weeks. It is said that the Duke of Windsor and Mrs Simpson were guests, for it was a great place for people who shunned publicity. When The Beatles were appearing in Plymouth they chose the island for their headquarters. But without doubt the most famous visitor of all was Agatha Christie who came for many frequent, short, but refreshing stays. Two books she wrote whilst staying here were *Evil Under the Sun* and *Ten Little Niggers*, now changed to *And Then There Were None*.

Evil Under the Sun was published in 1941 and the influence of the island is very obvious in the story. A map at the front of the book bears an uncanny resemblance to Burgh Island. It has a similar shape and is set in an almost identical position to the alignment of the coast. However, there are some less subtle differences. A causeway of concrete exists on Christie's 'Smugglers Island', one that would in reality have resembled a dam stretching across the sea. The hotel was the 'Jolly Roger Hotel' and Bigbury Bay was 'Leathercombe Bay' for this Hercule Poirot story. Agatha Christie emphasised that the island was the perfect place to 'get away from it all,' which, of course, is all very well provided there aren't too many murders taking place!

The hotel has enjoyed a rebirth under the Porters and won awards, one of which, in 1993, acknowledged their efforts to re-create its original magic. The Good Hotel Guide presented an award that stated: "For recreating, with panache, the high life of the '20s."

Although the island is privately owned, there is access but no public right of way to the top of the hill. There are lovely walks among the bracken, wild poppies, the squill, which is a rare and beautiful pale blue blossom in spring and early summer, and the crimson purple pyramidal orchid. The path to the hotel is flanked by palms and scarlet fuschia.

Not quite so welcome, was a colony of rabbits, which moved back to the island and dug up the croquet lawn! But in spite of this, the return of wild life is looked upon as a good omen in re-creating the enchantment of the 1930s.

On Little Island, which is connected to the main one by a steep, narrow path, is a natural bird sanctuary for herring gulls, cormorant, kittiwakes and other sea birds. From the huer's hut it is possible to look across the bay eastwards to Bolt Tail, or westwards over Rame Head, which lies beyond Plymouth. It is like being on top of the world with a clear view of sea and sky, with only the sea birds floating on the thermals for company.

Bigbury-on-Sea and Bigbury

And so across the causeway to Bigbury-on-Sea, a settlement with a permanent population of about three hundred. At the end of Queen Victoria's reign Bigbury-on-Sea was virtually non-existent with the road to the coast petering out at Mount Folly Farm only to become a rough track down to the shore. About 1910 the first houses appeared and between the wars there was a steady rise in the number of properties. The list of residents included an extremely high proportion of doctors who saw that these houses were a good investment and, at the same time, extolled to convalescing patients the wondrous recuperative qualities of the sea air and the fine water supply! They were quite right as the sea air at Bigbury-on-Sea is indeed exhilarating and would probably make anyone feel a lot better.

The main complex of tourist buildings, partly derelict, at the top of the slipway leading down to the beach, once catered for the needs of the visitors but originally was used for other activities. They began life as curing cellars for the pilchard trade but that

industry declined and the place fell dormant. However, as the combustion engine opened up the countryside and the coastline to greater numbers of people, Mr Stevens, of Modbury, converted the site into a bus depot. Eventually the complex evolved into a cluster of buildings, which included the appropriately named Tom Crocker Inn. There was even a sort of mock Cornish fishing village housed in this unattractive building but it was a poor, unconvincing, imitation and was garish in the extreme. The buildings have become unsafe and at the time of writing, await their fate in a truly dilapidated fashion. Years ago their gents toilets raised a smile or two as they were adorned by the sort of

mirrors found in a Hall of Mirrors at a fair. Consequently one's visit there was a visually amusing spectacle. However all the necessary needs of the visitor are now catered for in buildings close by – quite possibly where you bought this book!

The scene at Bigbury-on-Sea might have been transformed in other ways had the ambitious plans of the railway builders reached fruition. A line was constructed from Plymouth to Yealmpton and another had been taken from South Brent down to Kingsbridge. The grand plan was to link Yealmpton to Kingsbridge making it a through route with a branch line, from the Modbury area, running down to Bigbury-on-Sea. Had it opened it would surely have mushroomed the growth of this seaside community. Finances and practicalities meant that these grandiose plans were shelved.

High on the hill above Bigbury-on-Sea, Archibald Nettlefold started up what is now known as the Bigbury Golf Club. Basil Perry, the Secretary, explained that the property over which the course extends, belongs to Evans Estates of Cardiff, who probably bought it from Nettlefold in the first instance. However some years ago they were organising a charity match and wrote to GKN (Guest, Keen and Nettlefold) asking them to act as sponsors, as Archibald Nettlefold had originally been a founder member of Nettlefold's Screws, as the firm then was. They replied that they had never heard of him! However, the Club still play for a Nettlefold Cup.

Rumour has it that in 1936 when Archie sold the island because of his approaching blindness, he also sold the golf course to twelve members on condition they formed a limited company with £100 contribution from each of them. However, the only names on file were Arthur Pearce and Percy Fletcher in 1945, and earlier, in 1923, Ernest Frank Anthony, Solicitor, and Charles Edward Evans, Gentleman of Nailsea. Perhaps this was the original Evans who was a keen golfer himself and anxious for the course not to fall into the hands of the developers.

The golf course is built on top of the cliffs and overlooks Bigbury-on-Sea and Bantham whilst, inland, the hills of southern Dartmoor can be clearly seen on a fine day. The exposed nature of the course, to the elements, has resulted in one that possesses few natural trees. To combat this, thousands of trees, of differing species have been planted in and around the course. Alas very few have survived. It has been found that the only type to thrive is the Monterrey Pine, chosen because it grew well in similar conditions on the Scilly Isles.

Bigbury-on-Sea and Bigbury are two separate communities. The latter, which can be seen from the golf course, is a hilltop village about one and a half miles inland. St Lawrence's in Bigbury is mainly fourteenth century but was rebuilt in 1872. There are fine brasses in the northern aisle and a side chapel with two brass effigies on the floor commemorating Joan, the first wife of William de Bykebury, and their only daughter, Elizabeth.

William was the ninth and last in an unbroken family line who settled in Bigbury, from where they took their name, in the reign of King John. Elizabeth is shown in a flowing mantle and mitred head dress with two dogs at her feet. She was married twice, to Sir Thomas Arundel of Tolverne, High Sheriff of Devon in 1438, and later to Robert Burton, also a High Sheriff of Devon in 1451. Part of the ancient family house remains and can be seen close to the church together with a dovecote of great age in the orchard, a symbol of the de Bykebury's importance in Royal eyes.

The church contains a lectern that has an interesting story to tell. Several centuries ago it was a gift from the Bishop of Exeter, Bishop Oldham, to Ashburton's church. As the Bishop's personal symbol was that of an owl, the lectern was in this creature's form. In the nineteenth century, Ashburton sold it to Bigbury for the princely sum of eleven guineas. When the locals saw it, they were not very pleased with its design and so had the poor owl's head removed. This was replaced by an eagle's head, which now rests proudly on top of the owl's body.

St Ann's Chapel

Up the road you come to the cross roads and the hamlet of St Ann's Chapel with the Pickwick Inn, part of a fourteenth century chapel. When a blocked up wall space was opened up during alterations to the house in the 1930s, a chest containing old books and documents was found but someone threw it on a bonfire! However the house remains, a remarkable home with a bedroom in the chapel itself. Here too, was a meeting place for the Royalists in the area who gathered support from the neighbouring manor houses.

St Ann was a Celtic goddess famed for her partiality for babies as a delicacy in her diet! The decapitated heads were thrown into her wells and skulls have been found as evidence. The church used to legitimise pagan saints by building churches on their religious sites, including so called holy wells, so perhaps this is what happened here.

Ringmore

Ringmore is partly hidden below its church of All Hallows from where, on a clear day, you can see Eddystone lighthouse. The building of the church today is virtually that which stood here in the thirteenth century, with some parts going back to Saxon and early Norman times. The sundial above the porch however is eighteenth century.

Ringmore is a small village situated on a hill about half a mile from the sea at Ayrmer Cove or Challaborough, whichever is your preference. The village may be small but in the past has bred some big hearted priests.

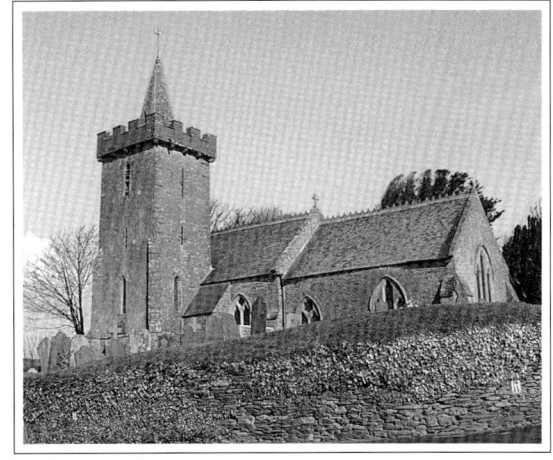

William Lane was the Rector when the English Civil War disrupted life in Devon between 1642-1646. He was a staunch Royalist who firmly believed that prayer was not enough and that action was necessary. He stirred the men of Ringmore from their slumbers and trained them for the King. On high land that he owned at Aveton Gifford he set up a cannon that was strategically located to guard the bridge over the River Avon. On one occasion when the Parliamentarian forces marched on Salcombe he had no hesitation in firing on them, an escapade that singled him out as a prime target for revenge. This incident earned him the nickname Bishop Lane (which he wasn't).

    Boatloads of men were sent from the Parliamentarian garrison at Plymouth with express orders to take him and hang him immediately from the nearest tree. These men landed below the village at Ayrmer Cove but had been spotted just in time. Lane hid in his church and was lucky that it possessed a secret room, complete with chimney. The Roundhead troops first searched the nearby Rectory, seizing Lane's two sons. They were taken back to Plymouth as prisoners of war and given a hard time because of their father's involvement in the war. Lane's sheep, cows and hens were also taken but this is understandable as Plymouth had been under siege and there were starving people in that town. The inevitable search of the church did not uncover Lane's hiding place. For three long months he holed up in the small secret room. Brave local people showed their loyalty to their rector by risking their lives to bring him food each night.

Eventually, when the coast was clear, Lane made his escape across the Channel to France, where he worked until the war ended in England. Being an industrious fellow he quickly made enough money to enable him to negotiate an agreement with Cromwell, and he returned to his land and property at Aveton Gifford at the head of the Avon estuary. Here he owned mills but his successor as rector, a gentleman called Barnard, had not only usurped his position but had also embarked on a mission to destroy Lane. His first deed was to cut off the water supply to his mill. Lane and his family got fed up with the treatment and moved to Torquay where Lane worked as a quarryman, but Barnard pursued them across South Devon and made life so difficult that drastic measures were called for.

Sixty-three-year-old William Lane decided that life was not being fair to him so he set out and walked all the way from Torquay to London, a distance of just over two hundred miles, to confront Cromwell's council with his plight. He received a fair hearing and was given the authority to appoint his own successor as Rector and dispossess Barnard of the title. With this victory he left London to return to the West Country.

When he reached Exeter, Lane stopped to take refreshment but drank contaminated water. He developed a fever and within a few days he died. He was buried in Alphington, just a few miles outside Exeter, an ignominious end for a stalwart trooper who fought many battles only to succumb to a minute but fatal germ.

Just over two centuries later there was more trouble and strife to shake rural Ringmore from its sleepy ways and again it was a Rector who led the charge, but this time purely for the sake of his religion. Shortly after 1860 the Rev Hingeston (who in 1868 became Rev Hingeston-Randolph) was involved in a heated argument with five local dissenters. They claimed, wrongly as it transpires, that there was fighting during the church service on two consecutive Sundays. In a long and beautifully written letter to the local press, the Rev Hingeston severely castigated the dissenters giving extremely explicit reasons why they might have had cause to start a war of attrition. Of the various charges he replied, "I am sorry to be compelled to say that it is, in every single particular, an atrocious lie. On the 21st Ult, after service, a poor misguided fellow rushed into the church and struck and collared the Sexton because the latter had corrected a boy (his son) for throwing apple cores about the church. As for the priest, I never 'collared' anyone, or put anyone out of this or any other church (during divine service) in my life. I did put the man who assaulted our Sexton out of the church on the occasion alluded to, as I was in duty bound to do."

This was the beginning of his time as Rector and obviously it didn't unsettle him for he stayed to serve the parish for fifty years. In that time he transformed an almost ruinous church into a lively one, which was greatly enhanced by his changes and presence. His improvements included the removal of a rickety old minstrels' gallery, which had occupied the west wall of the nave, and the original circular window was replaced. It is said that in smuggling days a light would shine from here to guide ships to Ayrmer Cove.

In the 1950s repairs were carried out to the west wall of the nave revealing a Gothic window or door reaching from just under the rose window to the ground. Whilst the scaffolding was in position, the weathercock, which had been used for target practice and had seized up, was replaced by an exact copy. The rector wrote in the records that, like Longfellow's weathercock, this one:

"Can see the roofs and streets below and the people moving to and fro,
And beyond without roof or street the great salt sea and the fishermens' fleet."

Ringmore is an enchanting village of fine cob cottages with flower filled gardens and two old farms, also the Journey's End pub, an old smuggling inn where R.C. Sheriff wrote his play of that name. In 1929 the Elmhirsts of Dartington financed the play described as the most wonderful play ever written. On their advance of £400 they made a profit of £1,500 a week. In the lounge an autographed copy of the first production's playbill proudly hangs on the wall. The building was constructed as accommodation for the labourers who built Ringmore's church in 1180. In the reign of Queen Elizabeth I it became the New Inn and it is believed that it was one of a chain of inns, all approximately 16-18 miles apart, where teams of packhorses could be rested. The distance was regarded as the 'going rate' for a day's travel.

Challaborough

Challaborough lies on the coast just under half a mile to the south of Ringmore, just over the cliff from Bigbury-on-Sea. Although it is little more than a hamlet, its curving sandy beach draws people like a magnet. This once quiet, but still lovely, beach has been

transformed into a popular resort in miniature, with hundreds of caravans lining the valley sides peeping over each other to get a glimpse of the sea. The hamlet has no church of its own and grew from a row of coastguard cottages. Originally deliveries of provisions to this small community often came by sea because inland communications, which bordered on the primitive, made travel by land an irksome task.

Kingston

Kingston is a small village, with many beautiful thatched cottages, perched on a hill high above the Erme Estuary described by Raymond B. Cattell as "at the end of all creation." However, some people find that to be a positive attraction, none more so than some of the television personalities who use the village as a retreat. Despite having a population of only a few hundred, the village has its own fire engine!

The Dolphin is one of the most celebrated pubs in the district and has the distinction of a road running right through it. This can be simply explained in that it has buildings on each side of the road. The cellar of the sixteenth century main building was once a fish store, the catch having been brought up to the village by donkey. On the opposite side of the road is the Tallet Bar (Tallet is an old Devonshire word for a hayloft). At the turn of the century it was used as the village dance hall, and no doubt many lasting relationships have been forged here.

The Erme Estuary and Mothecombe

The stretch of coastline from Bigbury-on-Sea to the mouth of the River Erme at Mothecombe is a striking one in the early morning sunshine. The great grey cliffs shine so brightly that they bear a resemblance to the famous white cliffs of Dover! However the geology is different and the coast path along it is a demanding one. With a strong offshore wind, strolling along can be a daunting prospect. However, if the spirit of adventure and the necessary energy reserves are available, it is a splendid, up and down, exhilerating walk.

There is a crossing place across the mouth of the Erme, at Wonwell, at low tide only, but even then care should be taken.

The Erme rises on Dartmoor in a notoriously wet area of mire and bog but soon gathers enough momentum to carve out one of the loveliest valleys in Devon. Between Dartmoor and the beginning of its estuary, just west of Modbury, it flows through a patchwork quilt countryside of fields and woods with footpaths and roads keeping company with it.

The Erme estuary is now a site of Special Scientific Interest and is also designated as an Area of Outstanding Natural Beauty – both titles are equally deserved for the stretch of water from Sequer's Bridge to the sea is exquisitely beautiful and unspoilt. The adjacent lands on both sides have been under the same ownership, the Flete Estate, for over a century and they have made a determined and successful bid to preserve the estuary's peaceful character.

There are no obvious ports on the Erme Estuary probably because its mouth is so shallow. Many dangerous rocks also prevent larger vessels from entering. A relatively deep water channel exists, which boasts a soft sandy bottom, but navigating it is another matter. However, Raymond B. Cattell in *Under Sail Through South Devon and Dartmoor* had no such problems in his two-man canoe and says of the experience:

"*I am irrevocably convinced that it is the loveliest river in Devonshire, and therefore in England. Its mouth, like that of the Avon and the Dart, hides shyly between lofty hills, but as one enters it smiles at one with fair wide beaches, indeed, the deep cove of Mothecombe would make a playground for a City. In a little while the shadowy woods begin on either side and continue in unbroken perfection as far as one may care to navigate.*

"*Soon we went carefully owing to the many sandbanks and the tortuous sweeps of the Channel, which kept us constantly guessing. Never have I seen so many varieties of sea birds as on these sandbanks, it is a perfect bird sanctuary ...*" Ray Cattell continued up the Erme to seek out a camping site, which presented him with an exciting adventure.

In the eighteenth century there was an additional ridge of sand and shingle that projected from the western side of Erme Mouth across the mouth of the river. It was used for a fair, which was an annual event on the local calendar. The work of the winds and tides have worn this feature away.

There were some grave moments for the Erme Estuary and Mothecombe in May 1990. Eighteen miles of the Bigbury Bay coastline became awash with crude oil from the gigantic Liberian-registered super tanker *Rose Bay*. Even though visibility was down to six miles in hazy conditions, the Brixham-based *Dionne Marie*, with its five-man crew, should have avoided collision, some fourteen miles south of Start Point, with this immense vessel, 1,100 feet in length and as high as a multi-storey building. That unfortunate collision, on Cup Final afternoon, had awful consequences for this coastline as an 80 square mile slick threatened the flora and fauna of the Bigbury Bay shoreline, also the economic prospects of those who derived their livelihoods from tourism. Eleven hundred tons of crude oil poured from the punctured tanker and booms were set up across the mouth of the Erme Estuary.

Five wartime Dakotas and two Cessnas were brought in to pour dispersants on the slick and an army of workmen were brought down to clean up the aftermath, a sickening black sludge that did a lot of damage. After a major operation, which some thought was inadequate, Bigbury Bay returned to some semblance of normality although the 'scars' were visible for ages afterwards.

The Chairman of the West Country Tourist Board, mindful of the need to protect the economy of the immediate area, attracted a lot of publicity by bathing in the sea at the end of May to show that the area was recovering and that potential visitors should not be put off.

Mothecombe Beach is a private one but public access is permitted on Wednesdays, Saturdays and Sundays. There are carriage drives beside the estuary but permission to walk along them has to be gained by writing to the Flete Estate Office at Mothecombe.

However, there is no need to seek permission to walk the coastline to the west of the Erme's mouth and it is an experience well worth the effort. Walking westwards is invariably harder than walking eastwards as the prevailing wind can impede the walker's progress if it's in its full fury. Should you wander along this western extremity of Bigbury Bay you will have the outcrop of St Anchorite's Rock in sight for the first mile or so. It is believed to once have been an abode of a hermit of that name. From a distance it is impressive but from close quarters it is a disappointing rock. Farther on, at Beacon Hill the coast walker will encounter Revelstock Drive (known in the past as the 'Membland Drive'). This is named after the first Earl of Revelstock who had this route cut out of the cliff as a carriageway. His home was nearby Membland, which, alas, has since been demolished. At one time it entertained members of the Royal Family and several famous people have passed along this bit of coastline in carriages.

Ever since its opening in the 1880s local people used this carriageway for their outings, but it was always spelt out that it was then not a public right of way. Signs stating this were found along the drive and Lord Revelstoke would close the path on one day every year to establish his control.

Now the route, engineered by local fishermen, is ideal for a gentle, easy on the feet, ramble on towards Newton Ferrers and Noss Mayo but that will have to be another book and another day! Burgh Island was meant to be the centrepiece of this publication so we will return to the mouth of the River Avon, which bubbles its way out to sea just to the west of the island and then examine the eastern side of this splendid bay.

Bantham

Beautiful Bantham or Bantham Ham lies at the mouth of the Avon, one of the few places on the South coast of Devon where there are sand dunes. At one time this small port was a hive of industry with sloops and barges a regular scene at its small harbour. At low water the fine flat sands were frequented by a small army of cockle-boys. Cargoes of limestone, artificial manure and coal were just some of the cargoes to be landed whilst this was replaced by outgoing corn, potatoes or other locally grown foodstuffs. Bantham even had its own pilot who would have to row out beyond the extensive sand bar to escort incoming or outgoing vessels. In between times he flexed his muscles to convey passengers across the river mouth from Bantham to the Bigbury side.

It is the sands that have attracted visitors from many a mile to visit Bantham. In Mr Fox's book about the Kingsbridge area in 1874 he states, with a great deal of enthusiasm: *"The sands on the beach at Bantham are the firmest for walking on of any we know in the neighbourhood and a great variety of shells (some of them rare ones) may be collected here. The rocks are capital for a scramble, and the deep rock pools, fringed with beautiful sea weeds and corallines, and tenanted by prawns, periwinkles, hermit crabs, sea anemones and many another creatures, most tempting to the collector for a marine aquarium, may occupy the afternoon very pleasantly on a long summer's day."*

Many local people prefer to call the Avon by its other name, the Aune. Slightly farther up the creek is the hamlet of Aunemouth, which was called Aunamouth or Avonmouth in the past.

The Ham in Bantham Ham refers to the elevated plateau of heath covered vegetation, which forms a high spit protruding across the mouth of the Avon. Originally a pre-Roman camp existed here. It had natural defensive advantages with water on three sides and a marsh on the fourth. It was 'discovered' in November 1703, when the sands that now cover it were temporarily removed to reveal it after one of the worst storms ever known.

During that same storm, Henry Winstanley, eccentric builder of the first lighthouse on the Eddystone Reef, was drowned when his strange-looking edifice was destroyed. Alas he had boasted that it would withstand any storm and had gone out to visit it to see if it would. For those with good eyesight, the present tower on the Eddystone reef can be seen on the horizon, from most points of Bigbury Bay, on a clear day. In more recent times the Ham has been used for sheep grazing whilst they were kept company by a vast population of rabbits.

Behind the Ham is the old thatched boathouse on the salmon quay, known locally as Jenkin's Quay. This boathouse is probably the most photographed feature on the coastline between the Dart and the Plym. It appears in guide books, on calendars, and postcards because of its colourful appearance against such a lovely maritime backcloth. Today it is a private residence but in the past it has been used to store fish or as a salting station when pilchards abounded in the bay.

Many former guide books stated that Bantham had two inns. It doesn't! The only inn is The Sloop, a sixteenth century edifice, which was once owned by the notorious smuggler, John Widdon, who also plundered wrecks on the Bigbury Bay coastline. His 'stingo' (illegal imported liquor) was stowed away at the village smithy or on the porch roof of Thurlestone Church! In the past the inn minted its own coins, an early form of tokens, enabling customers to use them to good purpose at Bantham. No denomination is given so the value of 'one' or 'one and a half' is not known.

The Avon Estuary

An estuary is the part of the river that is tidal and in the case of the Avon it is tidal roughly as far as the bridge at Aveton Gifford, about four miles upstream. As was common with almost every other river in Devon, limekilns were located on the banks of the Avon at Stiddicombe Creek, Hexdown Quay and at Bantham. Most of the lime came from quarries in the Plymouth area and the burnt lime, which had to be used quickly, hence 'quicklime', was used as a sweetener to improve the soils.

One of the most unusual roads in England exists along the west side of the Avon's estuary. For over half a mile it is possible, if the tide is right, to drive along level with the water. In places where the road becomes submerged, marker posts show the way ahead so as to prevent any erring motorist from disappearing into a sea of mud. Dave Clark, in the film "*Catch Us if You Can*" filmed some watery sequences along this road. Typical of filmmakers, it was cut in such a way that in the first glimpse they were seen heading towards Bigbury at the end of the tidal road, and in the next shot they were half a mile back heading in the same direction. However, despite this editing, they still made it safely to Bigbury-on-Sea.

The valley of the Avon's estuary is deep and steep running almost north-south. With the prevailing wind being a westerly one it means that the Avon's waters or mudbanks are sheltered havens that receive visitors of many kinds. The marshes and the muddy creeks provide a food source that can sustain a healthy bird population of wading birds and wildfowl. With such prime conditions for insects, and some of the lower forms of life, an intricate food chain exists. Birds of many species can be spied in this estuary and amongst them are teal, mallard, lapwing, curlew, plovers, dunlin, shelduck, sandpiper and many more.

Probably the best way to appreciate this wondrous variety of wildlife is to slowly sail up the Avon. Although Raymond B. Cattell ventured up in 1934 it has changed little since that time. In *Under Sail through South Devon and Dartmoor* he describes Bantham and the Estuary as follows:

"*Bigbury Island has a finer appearance from the sea than from the village, but we had little time to scan it, for we had to cross the bar at the mouth of the Avon with an inrunning tide and the wind against us. There is a broad gap to the left of the breaking water and through this we sailed easily and came anon in sight of Bantham. Bantham is a pretty, whitewashed, open village, quite unspoilt, and a resort of small-boat yachtsmen who were even then enjoying their weekly regatta in the swift current and blustering wind.*

Burgh Island before the present hotel was built

"*There seemed to be a likely camping place in the flats by the ferry, but we decided to take advantage of the tide to explore further up the stream. Almost at once the land locked to, with the finality of interlocking teeth, leaving us as if in some mountain lake. The Avon, like most of these rivers, has its own unique character of beauty. Winding shyly among vaulting hills as high as those of the Dart, it seems cut off from the rest of the world and, indeed, practically no building is to be seen anywhere in its kingdom. It has the charm of utter virgin innocence. Where the stream divides we landed on the central rocky point, with an old limekiln 'castle' and a steep bracken-covered hill behind. From this camping ground it seemed inconceivable that we had ever been to sea: two more hills had crossed their arms between us and the ocean, whilst around were farms and woods and the quiet arms of the lake. Wild birds of the estuary wheeled and called around us.*"

Thurlestone and its Rock

This is a lovely village of quaint thatched cottages many of them garlanded with roses, fuschias and woodbine. It is located on rolling hills about a quarter of a mile from the sea. Its popularity with holidaymakers has prevented a population decline that has been common in other parts and villages of the South Hams.

Thurlestone derives its names from the distinct feature of Thurlestone Rock, which stands almost stubbornly resisting the might of the sea whilst all around it has been worn away. Indeed the locals have noted this resistance and have applied some homespun wisdom or advice into the expression "Brave every shock, Like Thurlestone's Rock".

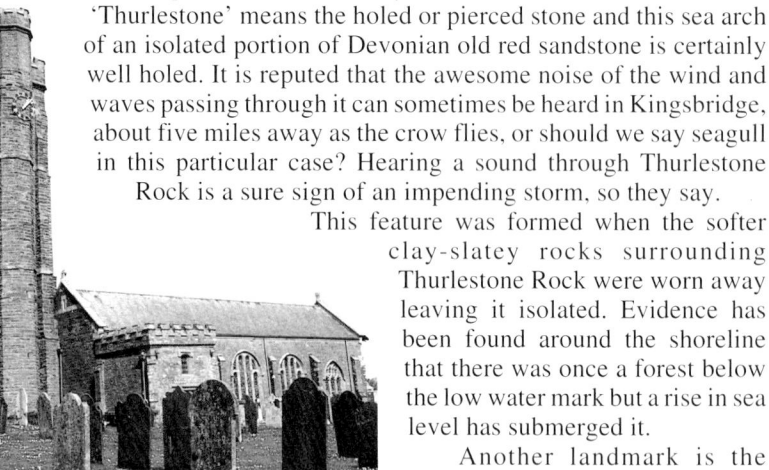

'Thurlestone' means the holed or pierced stone and this sea arch of an isolated portion of Devonian old red sandstone is certainly well holed. It is reputed that the awesome noise of the wind and waves passing through it can sometimes be heard in Kingsbridge, about five miles away as the crow flies, or should we say seagull in this particular case? Hearing a sound through Thurlestone Rock is a sure sign of an impending storm, so they say.

This feature was formed when the softer clay-slatey rocks surrounding Thurlestone Rock were worn away leaving it isolated. Evidence has been found around the shoreline that there was once a forest below the low water mark but a rise in sea level has submerged it.

Another landmark is the Church of All Saints at Thurlestone, a distinctive edifice of grey local slate. During the English Civil War its rector, John Snell, was heavily involved with the action. He was chaplain to Charles I and stayed with the Royalist Garrison in Salcombe Castle. At the end of the conflict articles of surrender were drawn up and one of the conditions, concerning him, was that he should be allowed to continue his living as Rector of Thurlestone. However the local population of Puritans decided to wreak their revenge on him by plundering all his worldly goods and twice stealing all his farm stock. The Rev Mr Snell took the hint and left the parish only returning many years later to see out his days in peace there, such is the magnet of this lovely countryside and coastline.

One nineteenth century rector helped to maintain and promote a teetotal environment. According to Mr Fox, in his guide book to the area, he states, *"It is worthy to remark that in neither Thurlestone nor Buckland (as is the case with South Milton) can you find a single public house. The Rector has, so far, been successful in his determination to prevent the opening of any place for the sale of strong drink; knowing well its demoralising effect on the rural population."* Fortunately today Thurlestone has the 'Village Inn', an important watering place that has had quite an impact locally.

The Thurlestone Hotel

The story of the Grose family, from humble beginnings, farming in the heart of rural Cornwall, to running one of the finest hotels in England, is a story of misfortune and perseverance.

It must have been quite a scene at Wadebridge railway station when, in 1895, Farmer William John Grose and his wife Margaret Amelia herded all their animals onto a special train to move to the South Hams. The move was very much a case of lock, stock and barrel with all their belongings and their four young sons. But life on the farm can be heartbreaking and Mr Grose had the cruel misfortune to lose most of his livestock through disease. The land owner then terminated the Grose's lease, a deed that was destined to change the fate of the whole family and their future lifestyle.

The Groses moved into a large farmhouse at Thurlestone. William and his wife had the foresight to see that the railway, which had brought them to the area, was also bringing large numbers of visitors, specially golfers. The first sign they erected said, 'Thurlestone House, Golfers accommodated, Picnic parties catered for, Terms moderate'. It is likely that the early success of the venture was thanks to Margaret Amelia's catering skills and the warm welcome given to visitors. Time after time whole families returned and the small hotel's reputation grew. In those early days all the guests sat down to eat at one long table.

Margaret Amelia's cream teas were also celebrated in the neighbourhood, perhaps even 'fit for a king'. It seems that whilst the Prince of Wales (Edward VIII) was a cadet at the Royal Naval College of Dartmouth he and a number of friends visited Thurlestone for a game of golf. Afterwards they repaired to the hotel for a cream tea. Rumour has it that the young prince was 'crowned' in a mock ceremony here, with either a waste paper bin or a chamber pot, by his colleagues. This is now the 'Village Inn'.

As time passed the hotel grew both in reputation and size with building extensions being added at regular intervals to cope with the ever increasing demand. At one stage an unusual record existed as every woman in Thurlestone was either employed, or had been employed at some time, in the hotel.

In the early days the hotel conveyed its guests from Kingsbridge's, now nonexistent, railway station by horse and carriage. William Grose had bought a fleet of carriages of various types, sizes and descriptions, which included broughams, wagonettes and Victorias. These could be hired by guests who wanted to tour the district. The innovative skills of the Groses lead them to be the first in the area to have a fleet of cars including a Studebaker tourer that was the envy of all for its ability to take the precipitous Aveton Gifford hill in top gear! However, the march of time saw to it that an ever increasing number of guests acquired their own cars and eventually the taxi service adapted by turning into a garage business.

The Second World War took its toll on the village, and the hotel. Two girls' schools from Eastbourne took over the hotel in 1940. Their stay was short-lived because, in the following year, the Royal Marines commandeered it as an official training depot. The Grose's home (they had moved to Kingsbridge) 'The Bungalow' became a hospital, so some of the present villagers can claim the distinction of having been born there.

The damage to the hotel was considerable. Some expensive dining room curtains were requisitioned and found to have been taken to Devonport to be cut up into dusters! Structural damage to the roof was caused because the leadings were not considered when a heavy anti-aircraft gun was located there. The military obsession for spotlessness meant that the greatly cherished polished floor was ruined and had to be renovated.

Following the war, petrol rationing continued until 1949. The isolated location of the hotel became a positive disadvantage and an anxious time followed. For a while the hotel was forced to close for the winter, a situation that continued until 1971. Since then the improved motorway system and an increase in wealth and leisure time has enabled the Thurlestone Hotel to thrive once again. It is now a luxuriously appointed, quality hotel set in a wonderful location. An unusual present day attraction in the hotel is a fireplace that was once the possession of Richard Adams, celebrated author of *Watership Down*. It is beautifully inlaid with rosewood and applewood.

Burgh Island and Bigbury Bay

Thurlestone Golf Club

This has to be one of the most beautiful golf courses not just in Devon but in England! Today it is possible to look out over soft green fairways and across the sweep of Bigbury Bay. It is hard to imagine what it was like about a century ago when the Thurlestone Golf Club was inaugurated in 1897.

This was a derelict stretch of coastline completely overgrown with scrub and brambles. It was known locally as The Warren and aptly so because a rabbit warren existed in the centre of the fifty acre site that had been earmarked for the intended golf course. Three men Dr Eliot (the local doctor) W.M. Beer (solicitor) and H.G. Prowse (brewer) were responsible for establishing a somewhat basic and crude course through an almost impenetrable jungle of vegetation. But once this prickly problem had been solved the club was launched with forty-eight very carefully selected members although the first clubhouse hardly befitted the social status of its members. They had to contend not only with continuously strong sea breezes narrow fairways and a vexing vegetation but also with sheep and cattle grazing on the course with thousands of rabbits scurrying about inflicting untold damage upon it.

The course was transformed after the Second World War when the beaches and scenery began to attract visitors again. The prosperity of the club enabled it to improve the facilities. Today the course covers much the same area, an open treeless cliff top course with soft springy turf to cushion the golfers' feet as they tramp around its 6,337 yards. One young holidaymaker who will long remember his visit to the course in 1974 was seven year old Harry Pratt who became the youngest golfer in Britain to achieve a hole-in-one on the sixth hole!

Hope Cove

Tucked away in the corner of Bigbury, lying almost snugly beneath the heights of Bolt Tail, is Hope Cove, which consists of Inner and Outer Hope. The latter is the modern little resort that attracts thousands to its beaches. In recent years the village has more than doubled its population despite a decline in its former main occupation, fishing.

Mr Fox of Kingsbridge, wrote a lovely description of this small community as he saw it in 1874.

"This usually quiet little cove sometimes presents a curious spectacle, from its being a sheltered retreat for wind-bound vessels, which occasionally lie there for a week, or more, at least, until the breeze is a favourable one. We have seen between fifty and sixty vessels lying at anchor, at the same time, within a limited space; and then the villages presented a very animated scene, from the influx of sailors, both foreign and English, who came ashore, and caused great demand for provisions of various kinds. Cart after cart arrived with butchers' meat and loaves of bread, and were as speedily emptied of their loads, with much laughter and vociferation. Then came the filling of water casks from the clean spring just in front of one of the inns; and the discovery of water-cresses in adjoining meadow. How they raced and chased, and vaulted over the stone hedge, and then came back again with caps, and handkerchiefs, and arms full of this wholesome and pleasant vegetable."

At that time there were only about one hundred inhabitants in total at Hope Cove and with local transport extremely limited in its range and scope, the village was dependent

(Opposite top) Thurlestone
(Opposite middle) Hope Cove
(Opposite bottom) Cottages at Inner Hope

upon hauliers and visiting traders for their daily needs. Although this applies to most South Hams villages and other rural areas of Devon, it is a fact that in terms of services, amenities and transport, Hope Cove was decades behind the more populated parts of the country. Visitors coming here from places like London must have felt that they were stepping back in time. However, many folk were quite glad of this state of affairs.

As with Burgh Island and Bigbury-on-Sea, the pilchard industry was important. The nature of the sea bed and the quality of water in the Bolt Tail area meant that crabs and lobsters, some of monstrous proportions, could be caught in great numbers. Before the First World War these were kept alive in storage pots in calm water beneath Bolt Tail until a vessel came by to collect them. Once aboard they were stored in the well of the sloop to keep them alive as long as possible until getting to market. Following the Great War the crab and lobster haul went by rail from Kingsbridge but the closing of the line and improvements in the motorway system mean that now they are transported by road to London, most ending up eventually in Spain (where the English go to end up looking like lobsters!).

The pots or baskets for catching these creatures of the deep were made locally. This was common practice and although the fishermen of Hope Cove didn't have the reed beds of the silted up creeks, like their counterparts in Start Bay, they did have a facility to buy from local farmers who possessed withy groves. This too saw change with better reeds from distant parts replacing local ones, only in turn for these to be replaced by man-made pots.

At the top of the slipway at Inner Hope is the old lifeboat station, which in its fifty-two year life span witnessed many moments of high drama. It was established in 1878 by the Grand Lodge of Freemasons; their emblem can be seen on the front wall, beside the emblem of the Prince of Wales. The royal connection continued in the name of the lifeboat (and its successors), *Alexandra* – the Princess of Wales. Hope Cove was a natural choice for a lifeboat station as Bigbury Bay and the high, rugged coastline from Bolt Tail to Bolt Head was a veritable graveyard for shipping. If a vessel was shipwrecked on this section of coast, it was certain that any rescue attempts would be most difficult and there are several recorded instances of daredevil deeds and amazing heroics by the local lifeboatmen in their attempts to save lives. Between 1878 and 1930, sixty-four people were saved by the various crews. The brave deeds were acknowledged by medals and occasionally by monetary rewards. The end for this small lifeboat station was signalled by the acquisition of a motorised lifeboat by the Salcombe Lifeboat Station.

Shipwrecks in Bigbury Bay

Stoke Point, just over a mile to the south of Newton Ferrers, is regarded as the western extremity of Bigbury Bay and, for the sake of this publication, Bolt Tail marks the eastern boundary. In between these lofty headlands the seas hold sway and this majestic sweep of coastline lies at the mercy of the elements. The coastline faces south west and the powerful prevailing south westerly winds frequently buffet the coast with all their might. Not surprisingly this has become a maritime scrapyard for ships with many stories of shipwrecks and tales of bravery abounding. Beyond Bolt Tail to the east, towards Salcombe, a vast number of vessels have foundered on the rocks beneath mountainous cliffs. (For more about this see *Around & About Salcombe*.)

The great heights of this part of the coast gave a grandstand view of the Spanish Armada in 1588. On Saturday 20 May thousands of spectators gathered on the cliffs of Bigbury Bay to witness the scene of 140 relatively large Spanish vessels in a crescent-like formation, going up the English Channel. However, several of the Spanish ships were chased completely around the British Isles including one of the two hospital ships, *St Peter the Great,* which went aground on 28 October 1588 on the Shippens at Hope Cove.

Almost everything from its wreck was salvaged, which led to some interesting improvisations. Just one example is a building called 'The Cabin' at Hope Cove, which is supposedly built from the timbers of this ship.

A French vessel, the *Commerce de Paris* chose to anchor in Bigbury Bay to see out a gale. She had come all the way from Brazil filled with such goods as cotton, tapioca and of course, coffee. With the 'wreckers' of South Devon anticipating a fruitful Christmas, for 1869, they gathered with interested and vested eyes as the ship gradually dragged anchor and went aground near the mouth of the Erme. Co-incidentally the sister ship, the *Paulista*, had suffered a similar fate, less than a year earlier, at Jennycliff Bay near Plymouth. The French captain wasted no time. Eight pistol-toting policemen were immediately recruited to guard the cargo, which proved to be a sufficient deterrent to the local wreckers.

Not so fortunate were two people from a vessel called the *Chantiloupe,* which ran aground in October 1757. A wealthy lady passenger managed to swim ashore only to suffer a gruesome death at the hands of the wreckers. She was heavily ornamented with expensive jewellery, which was seized from her in the most brutal fashion, some of her fingers being deliberately cut off to afford easy removal of the rings. Her ears were horribly mutilated as her earrings were torn off and, stripped and naked, she was left to die on the foreshore. A seaman, who also managed to swim ashore, was found buried on the beach. Since then other skeletons have been unearthed on beaches around Bigbury say so don't dig your sandcastle moats too deep!

Bolt Tail stands like a great rocky fortress, an awesome cliff that has witnessed many hopeless maritime situations. Numerous vessels have been driven against it, the biggest disaster of them all being that of HMS *Ramillies* (formerly the *Royal Katherine*), which went aground on this headland on 15 February 1760.

It was an unfortunate piece of navigation that lead to her fate. Her master wrongly believed that they were off the coast of Plymouth. Burgh Island was mistakenly identified as Looe Island, the skipper navigating east of this into what he believed would be the safe anchorage of Plymouth Sound. One of the crew had recognised this sweep of coastline as that of Bigbury Bay and tried to tell Captain Taylor. For his pains he was charged with insubordination and placed in irons. Thus the *Ramillies,* instead of sailing into the safe sanctuary of Plymouth, foundered on the towering walls of Bolt Tail. Out of a total of 734 on board, 708 people perished that day, with bodies and wreckage being washed up all along the length of Bigbury Bay. Most of the bulkier, heavier items that ended up in Davy Jones' locker remained with the mermaids and fishes for several decades until a local diver from nearby Hope Cove managed to recover several of them.

Films and Film Stars in Bigbury Bay

Bigbury Bay and Burgh Island have played a role in several films on a coastline that has also inspired several great writers to let loose their imagination. (If you wish to know more details of the many television programmes and films made in the county, you should read *Made in Devon* by Chips Barber and David FitzGerald.)

Supergrass was a full length feature film that used Hope Cove for the bulk of its shooting. In one scene Robbie Coltrane unflinchingly walked along the breakwater whilst quite large waves broke over him. Having walked along the top of this construction on a calm day, and having found it decidedly slippery, it makes Mr Coltrane's performance seem quite remarkable!

At the other end of Bigbury Bay, where the Erme pours into the sea, the sequel to *National Velvet* was made. *International Velvet* starred Tatum O'Neal, Nanette Newman, Anthony Hopkins and Christopher Plummer. This film's opening and closing sequences were filmed at Mothecombe with some superb aerial photography showing this stretch of coastline and, in the distance, the china clay pits on the edge of Dartmoor.

Between Mothecombe and Bigbury-on-Sea the great grey cliffs rise to alarming heights. The coast path passes along the edge of Scobbiscombe Farm where one of the most expensive films ever made in this country, had several scenes shot. In April 1985 Donald Sutherland and Al Pacino came to Scobbiscombe to 'shoot' a reconstruction of the Battle of Yorktown for the film *Revolution*. The enormous costs of filming were added to when a camera worth about a quarter of a million pounds, mysteriously 'fell' over the cliffs one night and was totally destroyed.

The legendary Kirk Douglas has also visited Bigbury Bay when, in 1975, he shot a scene for the film *Holocaust 2000*. The director was obviously aware of the rare tidal phenomena of an incoming tide on the two sides of the natural causeway to Burgh Island and used this to good effect. In the film the star had to run for his life to reach the safety of the mainland.

We thought it appropriate to end this little look around and about Burgh Island and Bigbury Bay with a mention of a film, from 1965, which also ended at the Island. It was the first film directed by John Boorman and followed the mid-1960s trend of featuring pop stars of the day in films. The *Magical Mystery Tour*, starring The Beatles, passed this way, as did the Dave Clark Five, a group from North London who made such golden oldies as 'Glad All Over' and 'Bits and Pieces'. However, this film was based on another of their hits.

In *Catch Us If You Can* (also titled *Having a Wild Weekend*) a group of youngsters flee to a lonely island in the West Country. They run across the sands to the waiting tractor (an earlier model with caterpillar wheels) and alight on a landing platform to look around the deserted hotel. Looking out of the window and seeing the smooth sands, covered with people, the heroine dismisses the Island with the words: "It's not even a proper island – it's just a gimmick in the sea!"

Hopefully you will disagree – if you are like us, you will find it is a very magical and special place.

OTHER OBELISK PUBLICATIONS THAT FEATURE THIS AREA:

The South Hams, Chips Barber	48pp	£2.50
Around & About Salcombe, Chips Barber	32pp	£2.50
Walks in the South Hams, Brian Carter	32pp	£1.95
Under Sail Thr South Devon & Dartmoor, R. B. Cattell	160pp	£2.99
Tales of the Unexplained in Devon, Judy Chard	48pp	£2.50
Made in Devon, Chips Barber and David FitzGerald	104pp	£2.99